The World
of
Wax

MIKE PEARCE

ISBN:10-1535024755
ISBN-13:978-1535024754

DEDICATION

This book is dedicated to all those who use wax and candles in their daily lives especially where they use candles to create an atmosphere of peace and remembrance. It is also dedicated to all those who work with wax as a craft to bring pleasure to many people.

MIKE PEARCE

CONTENTS

MIKE PEARCE

ACKNOWLEDGMENTS

The author would like to thank Christine Pearce for checking the manuscript. Also to those who introduced me to wax in its many forms.

1. INTRODUCTION

Ever since animals, plants and man existed, wax has played an important role. Today we take it for granted and either cover our bodies with it, eat it, or use it for special occasions. Wax in one form or other is produced from both plant and animal in many forms. Its waterproofing function, antibacterial and lubricant properties, as well as its aesthetic value, be it in hair or cosmetics, places it high on the list of essentials. Wax has helped us remember loved ones through effigies and given us a sense of the past history through wax works.

Candles are something special, often lit in remembrance of loved ones past and present. A candle said with a prayer will continue that prayer, it is said, until it extinguishes.
One must not forget the structural properties of wax, be it elaborate candles, honey

Comb, or numerous forms exuded from some insects. These far outweigh some of structures of the present day. We have used natural and manufactured forms of wax for years. We have mixed it with many chemicals, changed its colour and texture, added scent and increased melting points to meet our needs. We will still continue to do this for many years to come. So next time you find wax in your ears, remember it's there for a purpose as are the other forms of wax on this planet.

2. WHAT IS WAX?

Before the nineteenth century the word wax was
linked to bees' wax. The origin of this word comes
from the old English 'weax' from the honey comb of
the beehive.

Physically wax is seen as a naturally oily, heat sensitive
substance which is insoluble in water. Chemically it is
an organic substance made of long chains of
hydrogen and carbon.

Two types of wax exist. The first is synthetic made
from crude oil, alkanes and paraffins with no
substituted chemical group. Synthetic paraffin wax
can be large crystals with a fairly low melting point or
can be microcrystalline, branched or with cyclic
hydrocarbons with higher melting points.

The other kind is natural wax such as bees' wax.
These are similar to synthetic waxes but contain
substituted groups such as fatty acids, alcohols or
aldehydes in their structure. Bees' wax is more

expensive than synthetic waxes and can be extracted from honey combs in boiling water.

Many other natural waxes exist. Spermaceti wax from sperm whales, and lanolin from skin glands in sheep which is found in the wool. Insects produce natural wax over their outside surface and also produce other forms of wax. Plants also produce wax especially palms and many tropical and desert plants.

A fossil wax called Montan wax is found in fossilised lignin and brown coal. This wax, largely produced in Germany, has a high melting point of up to eighty degrees centigrade and can have asphalt and resin in it. A similar dark wax can be extracted from peat. There is also a mineral wax called Ceresin. This is whitish yellow, produced from ozocerite in soft shale and also has a high melting point. Waxes are flammable. Organic waxes like beeswax leave no residue when burnt. The formulations used in synthetic waxes are often secret.

3. AGRICULTURE AND GARDENING

Wax, due to its waterproofing properties, can be used in slow release pellets of fertilisers and insecticides such as pyrethroids as well as for poisons to kill vermin. The wax helps to slow down the breakdown of these products which could happen if directly exposed to light. It is also important for fruit growers and other growers for covering grafts of different plant varieties so as to keep out water and infection. Orchid grafts are especially susceptible to disease. The wax will also stretch once the graft has taken and the plant starts growing.

One can also use wax to seal cuts in trees or over the ends of the sawn branches. Waxes are often mixed with fungicides to protect the exposed tissue of plants and trees. Sometimes only the edges of major wounds are waxed allowing the rest of the surface access to air for self-healing.

Many commercially produced plants may be covered in wax around the base or roots to increase survival until purchase. Examples are lucky/double lucky bamboo and some orchids. Stems of roses may be covered with wax, as may their roots, to protect them before planting. The presence of wax on insects and plants can make it hard for chemicals to be effective when sprayed on them so wetting agents need to be added.

Wax can reduce oxidation which causes rusting so it's especially useful for spaying onto farm equipment or garden tools especially those stored during the winter. Wax is also useful in waterproofing clothing for use in the field. Hot pepper wax spray is used on plants, and acts as a repellent for squirrels and rabbits eating your plants.

4. ANIMALS AND PLANTS

Insects are some of the most remarkable wax producers. They have a layer of surface wax which covers their epicuticle (outer body). Insects also produce other forms of wax seen as tails or cotton wool like extrusions at the back. Worker bees have wax glands and produce wax combs when building up new colonies so there are more chambers for the eggs. The hexagonal cells constructed are economic on wax so bees use less energy in making them. It has been suggested that, like soap bubbles, when the wax is soft the cells are pinched into this hexagonal shape due to surface tension forces. The bees like termites, may have some way of judging distances. The comb cells contain young larvae, honey and pollen. They form wax from the sugars they collect and the more nectar collected the more wax is produced. The colour depends on the colour of the flower. The wax is secreted from glandular cells which grow longer with age. Queens and drones do not have these wax glands. The wax exudes onto paired, smooth, oblong areas called wax mirrors on the ventral part of the abdominal segments. These are abdominal segments numbered four and seven and the wax forms scales or flakes. The flakes produced are transparent and pulled out from the underside of the abdomen by the hind legs. The flakes turn white when chewed by the bees, and are built up like a wall one by one to make the combs. These can also include resins. Other bees can take the wax from the producers to build or repair the combs. The hexagonal cylinders of the comb fit side by side and are strong and a cap of wax is used to seal the chambers in the comb.

Wax secretion is only active for around twenty -one days and then the bees glands degenerate. The worker needs to eat loads of honey and they hang around the site of comb building. One to two pounds of wax are produced per hundred pounds of honey.

The homopterans; scale insects, aphids, and plant hoppers produce lots of wax which also contains resins and even proteins. The wax leaves their body through slits, pores or pore plates which mould the extruded wax into ribbons and tubes and other shapes.

The World of Wax

The psyllid Malaleuca, a tree pest in Florida, has many moulding structures and fine filaments are produced which merge together. In some insects, especially scale insects, slits and pits can also produce long ribbons, while other slits can produce short wax curls which are semi-circular in shape. Scale insects have amazing forms of wax secretions. Many are arranged around the area where balls of honey dew are produced at the hind end of the insect.

Shapes of wax from scale insects can be solid streamers emanating from tiny pores in thimble shaped structures. Wax can be produced either side of a structure in rows to meet round the other side to form a feather like structure. Scale insects can also produce other different forms from small curls of wax, hollow, circular or six sided hollow tubes to spiral solid tubes. These secretions can be produced, from structures at regular intervals. It is possible when the secretion stops that the wax produced instead of being tubes etc., becomes more liquid and forms platforms like floors in a high rise tower block. This floor is then lifted up by the new pillars of wax exuded and this is repeated again and again like a wedding cake of pillars then floors. Wax extrusions are mirrored in play dough kits where the dough is forced by a syringe type structure through various discs with different sized and shaped apertures. As with wax the extrusion reaches a certain size and height then drops back because of its weight only to be pushed up again or to the side by the extrusion of new dough. These turn down on the cuticle and break off into small curls. Often these curls are used to cover excretions such as honey dew produced by the insect so that the dew ball which can even be shot out, is no longer able to stick to the insect itself.

Wax also reduces attack by fungi and bacteria which is encouraged by the presence of honey dew. Sometimes the wax extrusion can creep up a spine like growing ivy. As in some fulgorids the plates of flower shaped wax glands with up to five to six hollow tubes wax production can also act as a protection barrier against enemies. Less wax is needed to be produced from pores if the insects are attended by ants who take away the sticky secretions. The cixidae like delphacids, as with some other insects, lay eggs on plant tissues or soil and cover them with wax. This forms a protection against predators and parasites until they hatch.

Insect wax is useful commercially. This can be a very productive industry but may need thousands of wax producing insects to get a couple of grams for use for polish and candles. Scale insects are farmed by Chinese wax farmers. They put the larvae on trees in bags with holes in.The whole tree then becomes covered with insects producing wax egg sacs and farmers then scrape the wax off the tree and can extract it with boiling water.

Some hibernating Lepidoptera such as Manduca sexta can have wax covering their pupa. This wax moth which can lay three to six hundred eggs in a bee hive, on hatching, can tunnel through the honey combs in a web. This weakens the larvae, removing the wax caps which can cause deformity in the new born bees. The pupa also has layers of wax on its surface.
Macroscopic hairs on the feet of some insects are

coated with water repellent wax so that they can walk on water.

 Zooplankton in oceans can store wax as esters for energy. This can be at high levels. Some can change their wax from saturated to unsaturated forms giving a tighter fit so that the organisms sink as the density increases. Even some bacteria have waxes which are in their body walls. Copepods use their wax as metabolic fuels. Wax is on the outside for protection and to stop desiccation.

Waxy secretions are produced from preen glands, (uropygial glands) a bilobed organ in the rump in caudal tract at the bottom of the tail feathers.in birds. This gives protection against wetting. The wax also makes the feathers flexible, and helps repel ants or parasites. Wax also gives ultra violet protection and protection from algae, fungi and bacteria.
Spermaceti wax from a sperm whale's adipose tissue is found in a large cavity in the head. In a cold environment it can be cooled so that the wax density increases which enables the whales to swim downwards. Spermaceti whale wax was used to define

the measurement of power of light, 'the candle'. This was light from seventy five grams of wax.

.

Plant wax.

Cutin is a fatty acid polymer on the outer side of plants, often mixed with other lipids to give epicuticular wax. Natural waxes have many functions in plants including waterproofing, protection from attack by animals, insects and the environment. As with insects wax can cover the whole surface but different forms of wax extrusion do occur as suggested by the study of the brassicae. (Cabbages etc.)

Wax also helps with the prevention or reduction of evaporation, and waterlogging or pollution. This is useful for plants growing by busy roads. Wax on plants may also cause insects to slip off as is seen in the pitcher plant with wax on its rim. This causes an insect to fall inside to be digested by the fluid contents of the plant. Water has powerful surface tension so forms spherical drops. Spread out papillae on leaves can mean droplets cling to them and not to the surface wax. Wax is hydrophobic and hates water so droplets roll off with dirt etc. This makes it difficult to use sprays on crops e.g. calcium to help with leaf growth. To apply any chemicals then a wetting agent has to be added to the spray or the droplets have to be electrostatically charged. Wax production is related to sunlight and can influence the polarity of leaves.

Wax also helps with the reflection of ultraviolet light which can be scattered by different crystalline crystals, shapes and chemistry found on the outside of leaves or fruits.

Wax is often visible on the surface of different fruits for example blue berries, bayberries euphorbia, Javanese figs, sumac berries, plums castor plants, rice bran, soya, tallow tree seeds, kalanchoes and broccoli. Usually the more wax the more mature the fruit or plant is. Some fruits have their own waxy bloom which can vary in amount depending on the fruit. However the visible appearance of wax e.g. on the surface of a plum does not mean there is more wax than on an apple, just that in the apple the wax is more transparent and less noticeable. Wax on fruit means they resist moisture, are more firm and experience less breakdown from oxidation. Rubbing a fruit such as an apple will get a shine from the wax. Apples still remain alive when picked. There is also the 'wax plant' a Hoya which has clusters of white or pink waxy flowers

Parts of plants and petals may have different waxes. Several palms are a good source of wax. Carnauba wax is a hard wax from the NE Brazilian palm fronds where it is mechanically scraped off and can be mixed with bee's wax. The ouricuri wax from the Brazilian feather palm is also scraped off leaves. Waxes can be found in shrubs such as euphorbia in Texas and Mexico (Candelilla wax) and also in the roots of jojoba. Esparta wax comes from reeds and is used in making paper.

One can spray fruit and vegetables with a fine thin layer of wax to prolong life and reduce the effects of oxidation from the air. Citrus fruits, cucumbers, and tomatoes are some examples. You can store apples for a year by reducing the oxygen but the fragile wax cover must be complete so that no fungi or bacteria can enter. The coating applied may also contain some fungicide. Some people are concerned that by applying a wax coat you are also trapping any pesticide previously sprayed under the wax.

5. ART AND SCULPTURE

The plasticity of wax and degree of hardness of the wax offers endless possibilities as does its water repelling properties. Cerography is the writing or engraving on wax. In ancient Greece wax tablets were hollowed out wooden rectangular trays which were then filled with a layer of wax. Words were written with a stylus and often the wooden tablet had a similar tablet which could be closed over the first so as to make sure the page was not destroyed or words deleted if exposed. . Wax tablets were still common in the Middle Ages. As the wax was soft mistakes could be removed by heating the wax surface or rubbing with the fingers.

Encaustic wax involves applying wax, often in different colours, using a brush to different surfaces, linen or thin wooden panels to form an image. Many Egyptian or Roman pictures were produced in this way and can be seen on display in the British Museum. Various tools were used to mould the wax, e.g. a cautarium (heated knife) and an acestrum (heated needle). Many pictures resembled people and these were placed on the heads of mummified bodies. The waterproof properties of wax are useful for painting. Recipes for making powdered wax paint also exist were wax was mixed with pigments and with oil or egg yolk to hold it together.

Other methods of using wax in painting are where the wax is applied to a surface or canvas with a crayon and then paint is applied around and on top. .

Wax is also applied to dyed material and at one time Dutch wax prints were produced followed by imitations produced from Indonesia. The Dutch on their way back to Europe found a market in Africa where the industry flourished. Patterns and designs then became personlised to different communities or figure heads. . Today prints from Europe can demand high prices. Dutch wax prints are now being mass produced by China and elsewhere.

Wax was also used for producing masks. In Rome death masks of the deceased were worn by relatives in the funeral procession. In London the Royal Society has a death mask of Sir Isaac Newton made in plaster with a wax coating. A wax death mask of Oliver Cromwell is housed in the British Museum. Colour can be added to death masks making them seem very realistic. In the Victoria and Albert Museum in Kensington there is a coloured wax relief named Time and Death by a Neapolitan nun, Caterina. This was created to help one think about mortality and to be displayed in a church. Here.in a graveyard Father Time points to a clock with a beggar on one side of it and various corpses are lying around.

Whole statues could be made of wax. Greeks and Romans used wax for statues to give the basic shape then used clay. The artist Degas used bee's wax in pellets with supporting rods with wax in layers and covering them with clay or plaster. One of his sculptures is the little fourteen year old dancer in wax, with a real bodice, stockings, shoes, skirt and horse hair wig. In the eighteenth century wax effigies of the dead person were placed on top of the coffin, especially if they were royalty. This proved a money spinner especially when these were then displayed in a tomb or sacred place and people were charged to visit. Westminster Abbey in London has a collection of British Royal wax effigies dating back to Edward III who died in 1377 and also a wax sculpture of Horatio Nelson. One hundred and forty wax figures with clockwork mechanisms were put on show in Fleet Street in the early 18th century

 In the church of Carmel Lisieux there is a wax effigy of Saint Therese in a glass case with golden sides. Her relics have been taken around the world and even to twenty to thirty cities in America. She predicted that after her death she would send a shower of roses upon the earth. In Russia a wax effigy of Peter the Great can be found at the Hermitage Museum, St Petersburg.

Human features are captured in the many wax work museums around the world. John Tussaud founded the wax museum in London and started modelling at the age of fourteen. Other parts of the world also have's museums such as in Beijing which is famous for showing Chinese people in history. Several Tussaud museums exist in America, also in Hong Kong, Amsterdam and Berlin. There is a Hollywood wax museum, National Wax Museum in Dublin, the Dreamland Wax Museum in Brazil and a national Presidential Wax Museum in Dakota. In India there is a Wonderwax museum and a celebrity wax museum. Madame Tussauds in London has characters from all walks of life including royalty, the royal family and murderers.

The Christian themed wax museum in Ohio has a bible walk with characters form the Old and New Testaments, the Heart of the Reformation, and a section on the Christian Martyrs. Daniel is even portrayed with lions in the lions' den. In Mysore India the wax museum has over a hundred wax statues of musician's from famous world bands or playing musical instruments.

Many people love to pose with the wax characters on display. However Nicki Minaj's wax figure at Madame Tussauds in Las Vegas had to be removed as several people were taking photos with indecent poses. It is quite common for people in costume to pose as wax figures and to surprise visitors when they move. In Madame Tussauds in America a genie from a Broadway show Aladdin, (Tony-winning, James Monroe Iglehart) and even Arnold Swartzinger from the Terminator pretended to be wax exhibits. It is also common to see a wax venus or sleeping beauty in a glass case with her chest moving up and down as if alive. Sometimes this is replaced by a live person to keep the public guessing if she is real or not. Most of the wax features are modelled from photographs these days but in the future 3D printers will be able to produce characters which are life-size and very realistic.

Wax can also be used for religious images. Chinese wax was used for temple images of the god of wealth one of the Buddhist messiahs. It is also in found in homes. Wooden painted Spanish statues were coated with wax, often for protection. One Catholic Church in Malta has a body of Gorg Peca a saint embalmed in wax and a separate body with his bones. During Egyptian times mummification orifices were plugged with wax or wax figurines included in the funery items.

The World of Wax

Temporary tattoos can use inkjet to print onto wax sheets in different colours. Tattoos are temporary. One can often use stencils and flip and rotate the drawing to reverse the image

Lost wax castings are used for casts in gold or silver, including jewellery. A wax model is produced and used to create a clay mould. Then the wax is melted out.

6. BOOKS,STORIES AND POEMS

A Life in Wax. Madame Tussaud by Kate Berridge. 2007.

Anne Frank -looks at how a single candle can both defy and define darkness.

Anthony Liccine-' If you devote yourself to God, then He in turn will continually stay with you, as an eternal flame stays with a wick, feeding off the overflow of wax; yet reshaping into something better'.

Aristotle –'we must no more ask when the soul and body are one then ask whether the wax and the figure impressed on it are one'.

Benjamin Franklin-' Parchment governs the world'.

Benjamin Franklin -'Pen, wax and parchment govern the world'.

Benjamin Franklin- 'If your head is made of wax don't walk in the sun

Bible KJV. Exodus 32-11. -Moses 'LORD, why doth thy wrath wax hot against thy people, which thou hast brought forth out of the land of Egypt'.

Bible KJV. Genesis 18:10-12 '-Therefore Sarah laughed within herself, saying, After I am waxed old shall I have pleasure, my lord being old also?'

Bible Daniel. 8.10.- 'And out of one of them came forth a little horn, which waxed exceeding great, toward the south, and toward the east, and toward the pleasant land. And it waxed great, even to the host of heaven; and it cast down some of the host and of the stars to the ground, and stamped upon them'.

Bible KJV. Genesis 41-56. -'And the famine was over all the face of the earth: And Joseph opened all the storehouses, and sold unto the Egyptians; and the famine waxed sore in the land of Egypt'.

BibleMatthew.24.12. - **Jesus Christ.** 'because iniquity still abound the love of many shall wax cold. But he that shall evidence unto the end the same shall be saved'.

Bible SV. Micah. 1-4-'And the mountains will melt under him, and the valleys will split open, like wax before the fire, like waters poured down a steep place'.

Bible KJV. Psalm 68-2. - 'As smoke is driven away, so you shall drive them away; as wax melts before fire, so the wicked shall perish before God!'

Bible ESV. Psalm 97-5. -'The Mountains melt like wax before the LORD, before the Lord of all the earth'.

Candle Wax Poems by Gloom Cloud. 'smile once more I am the melting wax candle'.

Champagne and Wax Crayons by Ben Tallon. 2015. Riding the Madness of the Creative Industry.

Chinese proverb –'The spirit of women is mad of quicksilver their heart of wax'.

Cities of Wax by Julie Closson Kenly 1935

Dan Brown- 'Please accept this humble fax, my love for you is without wax'.

Eleanor Roosevelt-'It is better to light a candle than curse the darkness'.

Ghanaian proverb-'You cannot kill an elephant with bullets of wax'.

Greek Anthology. Icarus son of Daedalus. His father made wings out of feathers to escape from Crete but

Icarus ignored the warning of flying close to the sun and the wax melted and he fell into the sea.

Gunpowder and Sealing Wax by Ann Lawson Lucas.1997.

Henry VI. Part 2 Act 4 scene 2. -'Some say the bee stings: but I say, 'tis the bee's wax; for I did but seal once to a thing, and I was never mine own man since'.

Jeremy Clarkson- 'Some say that he has no understanding of clouds and his ear wax tastes like Turkish delight. All we know he's called stig'.

John Calvin -Bible said to be twisted like a wax nose used by Catholics -Wax noses are a common prosthesis to cover a skin condition. Wax is cheaper than precious metals that were also used for this purpose.

Jonathan Swift (In battles of the books)-'. Instead of dirt and poison we have rather chosen to fill our hives with honey and wax; thus furnishing mankind with the two noblest of things which are sweetness and light'.

Keramos by Longfellow. 1893. (Poem) 'the moon will wane the mist and cloud will turn to rain'.

Les Dawson –'When I was a child I had wax in my ears. Dad didn't take me to a doctor he used me as a night light.

Leo Tolstoy (Anna Karenina).- 'The candle by which she read the book that was filled with fears, with deceptions with anguish and with evil, flared up with greater brightness than she had ever known, revealing her all that before was in darkness, then flickered grew faint and went out forever'.

Lewis Carroll - (Through the Looking Glass). 'The time has come the walrus said to talk of many things of shoes and ships and sealing wax –of cabbages and kings'.

Love Talk by Wendy Wax. 1997.

Little Ida Hans Christian Anderson. 1835. A wax doll series with a broad brimmed hat on her head much like the one worn by a lawyer.

Midnight Wax (Play) by Don Swartz.1974.

Night at the Wax Museum (Play and musical for schools) by Craig Sodaro. Lyrics Bill Francoeur **.2009.**

Night at the Wax Museum by Delilah Devlin. 2015.

Osceola by Thomas R. Stubbs.2010.

Plutarch- 'A soft wax is apt to take the stamp of seal so are the sounds of young children to receive the instruction imputed on them'.

Psalm 32.3. –'When I kept silence my bone waxed old through my roaring all the day long'.

Shakespeare (Hamlet Act 3 scene 1)-Their perfume lost, take, these again for to noble mind Rich gifts wax poor when given prove unkind'.

Secrets in Wax: Susanne by Banta Harper. 2009.

The Big Ball of Wax by Shepherd Mead. 1992. A story of tomorrow's happy world.

The Candle Wax Drops. Tryku poem translated from chinese. Imelda Senn. 2015.

The Christmas Tree by Charles Dickens 1850. 'Nor is the frog with cobblers' wax on his tail, far off; for there was no knowing where he wouldn't jump and when he flew over the candle and came upon ones hand with that spotted back-red on a green ground-he was horrible.'

The Design in Wax by Marc Book.1998 Cogan University Notre Dame on Dante Aristolian.

The Little Wax Doll by Norah Lofts. 1960.

The Story of the Wax Crocodile by Leena Maria.2016. A magician finds out his wife has a lover and makes a wax crocodile which comes alive and kills the lover in a swimming pool. His wife was also burnt and her ashes scattered in the pool.

The Story of the Wax Crocodile. Flinders Petrie from an Egyptian papyrus. 1899.

The Wax Man: a Latin American Story by Ola Loy; Raymond Ortiz Godfey.1994.

Through the Looking Glass. Walrus and the Carpenter by Lewis Carroll. 1872. 'of shoes of ship and sealing wax'

Wax Lips (Poem) by Cynthia Rylant. 2001. American life in poetry.

Wax On/Wax Off (helping pre-service teachers) Read Themselves, Children and Literature. Shelby A Wolf. Volume 140. No 3 2001.

Waxillium Ladrian-in a novel by Brandon Sandeson.

Wax in our World by Russell Solveig Paulsonhans. 1966.

Wax Trash and Vinyl Treasures by Roy Shuker. 2015.

Written in dead wax by Andrew Cartmel. 2016 (vinyl detective mysteries).

7. CANDLES

As soon as you light the wick of a candle the wax melts and rises up through the wick to reach the flame where it ignite to form gases, light and heat. Early candles were using combustible materials e.g. reeds rushes, or flax which had been coated or dipped in wax an example is found in ancient Egypt, using reeds placed in animal fat.. The Romans soaked papyrus in bees wax. In the Tang dynasty they used wax paper. In the Middle Ages bees' wax was preferred as it smells better. In the 18th century the tallow candle from shale oil was preferred as it was solid and would produce a good flame. Tallow fat came from sheep, also pig and cow but the candles gave a greasy, smoky flame and smell.

Joseph Morgan in1834 constructed the first candle making machine. Cotton wicks are the safest to use. Adding things can make the wax harder, raise or lower the melting temperature, or make them smell nice. One can create different compositions of wax to give less light and more therapeutic properties. The combinations can be seen in decorative candles, those used for time keeping, and for soft lighting for meals. Bees' wax does not mix with other things as easily. The use of paraffin wax and can cause allergies and cheap candles of paraffin wax can produce toxic fumes. Some candles emit soot and damage ceilings and walls. Candles can be used as timers with marks or pins placed in the side. Alfred the Great marked candles to see the passage of time.

Candles are also used in religious rituals. Churches used tallow, a hard wax for making candles. Cheap paraffin wax can contain pollutants and is often mixed with bees' wax for churches to get brighter and longer burning times Jewish tabernacles have seven branched candle sticks but originally used olive oil not wax. Rome had bees' wax candles for processions but later the pope withdrew processions in the Catholic Church. And candles were mainly just kept in the churches. The candles represent light, grace and beauty and appeared in church ceremonies. . Church candles often have 25% of bees' wax in them. The proportion of bees' wax in church candles is regulated by church law which also states the number of candles that can be present for different masses. Twenty candles are recommended for an exposition. Candles form an important part of Jewish tradition and rules surround the time to light the candle before Passover and the time of eating the evening meal as well as what to do if the candle is extinguished at Hanukah.

Ceromancy candle wax fortune readings have been in existence for over two thousand five hundred years. The reader may pray to God first and the drippings or forms when wax is dripped into water can provide answers to questions or by their shape predict the future. A recognisable shape in some cases can have a particular meaning e.g. a cat can mean a friend is untrue. Dropping wax into water is a Polish tradition on the day before St Andrews day. The wax is often poured through the eye of a key into the water. The future can be unlocked by this process and one can even predict if a girl will be engaged or marry.

The World of Wax

Candle power was the term used in the London Metropolis Gas Act in 1860. A standard 'candle' was use for photometry. Torches or spot lights can be labelled in millions of candle power.

Wax candles not produced from moulds are made by dipping a wick or taper in liquid wax which hardens and is then redipped. They can be dipped in twos or threes. Candles could have wicks of cotton, flax or hemp dipped in wax or rolled on soft wax. If they are too thin there is less light so dim, if too thick there is not enough fat to get good flame. Big candles have sheets of wax rolled around the wick. Tapers have thick, cotton wicks soaked in wax.

There are many hundreds of forms of candles from basic shapes to cupcakes, numbers and letters, buildings, cartoon characters, fruit, Christmas images and icons. Even wedding cakes can have a wax bride and groom in the centre both of them having wicks instead of heads. The containers holding candles also can be numerous many prevent draughts from blowing the candle out or causing irregular burning. One can also colour wax using specific wax dyes, water paints or crayons. One can darken the candles by increasing the amount of colour. Many hundreds of perfumes or aromas can also be mixed in with the wax to be released once lit.Perfumed wax flowers can be made by cutting petals out of wax with a pastry cutter, and curving them with the fingers and using sticky wax as a glue. . If fruits or flowers are made from wax one can use the relevant perfume and also dip the outside in another wax to get the natural colour. Often perfumes in candles can have useful functions. Citronella and Geranial oil can repel midges, mosquitoes and other insects. Jasmine or vanilla in candles in bedrooms are supposedly able to increase romance.

The Worshipful Company of Chandlers in London has registered different kinds of candle which early on included book candles for reading. Every town used to have a chandler (candle maker) and laws existed to prevent people making their own candles.
Moulded candles use PVC, rubber or plaster moulds to set the liquid wax. If glass is used one can get a shine on the outside of the candle. One can cut out or

add extra pieces of wax such as petals.
Embellishments also include cutting down the sides
of a candle and peeling these down and curling them
outwards.

Bees' wax is often not good as it sticks in moulds.
You can also use household items for moulds even
old tennis old balls. Wax can also be dropped into
water to create many different forms but you need to
make sure no water is held within the wax or it will
split. One can include objects or leaves in the wax and
can stick sections onto sides of candles or hammer in
patterns. Waxes can be painted with coloured wax, or
transfers can be used.

Wax is also used in lava lamps. As the liquid inside
heats up the wax at the bottom it melts and becomes
less dense and floats to the top and falls again when it
cools at the top of the lamp. It is also found in air
fresheners with essential oils, the aroma given out on
heating.

8. COSMETICS

Many cosmetics and creams contain wax. This keeps their creamy constituency. It also allows smooth application in lipsticks, eye liners, and eye shadow mascara and lip balms. Wax makes them thicker and retained longer. Wax can also hold other materials such as glitter.as seen in some lipsticks.

Bees' wax and plant waxes can keep an emulsion from separating out into an oil or liquid. This is needed for perfumes and fragrances. Wax is in moisturisers; unblock creams and powders applied to the skin.

Paraffin wax treatments have been around since the First World War. It is a heat treatment where parts of the body are placed in molten wax. The treated part of the body stays hot when removed and the skin is not shrivelled as happens in hot water. This wax treatment is used to treat rheumatism and skin complaints the wax forming a cast over the person's body. Even the whole torso can be covered in wax where applied with the person lying in a cradle. One can also spray the wax or paint it on the hands, feet or face. You can then peel it off. After waxing an area of skin you need to beware of the dangers of applying corrosive chemicals or heat.

Used waxing strips can be used for fortune telling. They can be photographed or sent off in the post. Different types/sizes of hair on the strip may be used as reference points and the density, distribution, patterns and colour can, as in tea leaf reading tell your fortune or answer yes/no questions.

Natural waxes also occur in many sun lotions and are favoured as they allow the skin to breathe.

Morticians are experts in using wax cosmetically to cover bruises and cuts on dead bodies. Even injuries can be addressed by using plaster and wax.

Wax also has a role in disguise and make up in the theatre and cinema. Spirit gum is placed on the face, and mortician's wax is used to build up features or construct scars etc. Greater amounts of wax are easier to apply to immoveable parts of the face such as cheekbones, the chin and the forehead. Professional wax is used for features such as cuts and scars and can be moulded on the skin using tools. It merges with the natural skin at the edges so as to look realistic.

9. DOLLS

Initially dolls were handmade from wood, clay or just sewn stuffed material. Wax came in in the 1700's and in the Middle Ages wax dolls were even made to hurt enemies often with part of a person's hair being used to represent them.. Before the eighteenth century wax heads were sewn onto cloth dolls at the shoulder. Three types of doll with wax heads exist, all with muslin or cotton bodies. The first heads were made in wax from plaster moulds and included glass eyes.

Animal or human hair could be fixed into the hair. The second type was a cheaper method from Europe. Here papier mache heads were dipped in wax producing a layer. There could be a slit in the centre of the top of the head. Where the hair was attached and styled into many different fashions. The glass eyes could be set awake or sleeping or could be changed using wires. A doll could also have reversible wax faces.

The third kind of doll used a mould but had plaster or cloth supports and sometimes inserts inside the head.

These inserts are useful for supporting structures such as the mouth or teeth. Using the moulding method dolls were exhibited at Crystal Palace in 1851.

Human hair was often inserted into the wax using hot needles. Madame Augusta Montanari was famous for her dolls and created wax baby dolls for royalty. With the wax dolls care had to be taken not to expose them to high temperatures as they could melt and they also had to be handled carefully if played with. Religious dolls were also very popular.

Medical dolls were created to illustrate anatomy. These were especially important where doctors were not allowed to touch female patients.so that the dolls could be used to indicate sites of pain.

10. EAR WAX

Ear wax (cerumen) acts as a protective layer over the ear membrane. It is found in the outer half of the ear canal and consists of secretions from sweat and sebaceous glands. Children have softer wax which has a lighter colour. Our ears, as with our skin, shed cells. As much as 60% of dead cells (keratin from skin) can be found in wax in the ear canal. The wax from over a thousand of these glands also has the antibacterial enzyme lysozyme in it which is also found in tears. This also kills fungi and bacteria and helps to repel insects. The wax, plus cells and enzyme, moves towards the exit over time and is carried to the exit. Moving your jaw helps to dislodge and move the wax outwards.

With ageing, or ethnicity wax can remain trapped in your ears. This can be made worse with the increase of hairs inside the ears with ageing. Ear wax commonly can block hearing aids.

Two kinds of ear wax are recognised. The dry form of wax is found in those living in colder climates. It originates from a recessive gene and in Asians and Native Americans can be seen as grey flakes wet and firm. In Japan it is called 'rice bran'.

The other dominant form is wet wax. If found in Asia it can be considered a disorder. Wet wax is more smelly and browner, and has more lipids (fat) and may contain a pheromone. This kind of wax is commonly found in African and European people. Wet wax has been called 'oily ear wax' or 'cat ear' wax.

Overproduction of earwax can be due to irritation caused by microorganisms or even illness. Often cleaning wax too regularly can initiate more production as can using hearing aids which may be recognised as a foreign object.

Homer's Odyssey records that candle wax was cut into pieces and was used by sailors to block off the songs of sirens who would lure them to their death in the sea.

.Many ways exist of removing ear wax. One way for wax removal which some believe is dangerous and ineffective is candling. and its use is restricted in many places. Candling involves lighting a hollow candle at one end and placing the other end in the ear canal. Heat travels down the candle to soften the wax. The fear is that some molten wax may enter and damage the ear.

Oils or peroxide can soften the wax. Irrigation, syringing .and cotton swabs (ear buds) are commonly used to remove wax but can compact the wax moving it towards the ear drum. These methods are more efficient for the dry flaky type but they may not be totally successful. Using micro suction with a microscope to see the wax present is much more efficient. A byotolaryngologist is the person who can deal with this.

Anything in the ear for long periods can stop wax movement to the outside; examples include ear bud headphones, excessive cleaning with cotton buds, or ends of hankies in your ear. Some people have used keys, paper clips, pen tops and hair grips to try to remove wax from their ears, but these can be dangerous causing infections or piercing ear drums.

Many animals, as with humans, have wax in their ears.
Baleen whales, which include the blue whale, can have
fibrous rods of wax in their ears which can be as long
as twelve inches long. The wax is laid down as layers
formed every six months and these form a record
like tree rings which can reveal their age, dry and wet
seasons, as well as the build-up of pollutants - for
example DDT and hormones.

11. FOOD

Wax is not poisonous and is not normally digested but passes through the gut. South African honey guide birds however do digest it using bacteria in their gut.

Wax can be found in the preparation of foods, in foods itself or used as a preservative Also wax can be used for coating materials that come into contact with food.

Preparation

Wax use in the kitchen is especially related to waterproofing. Wax can be used inside moulds t5o release prepared foods. It can be used in barbecue preparation. Cutting boards and salad bowls especially if made of wood can be waxed. Wax paper is moisture proof to keep food from sticking. You can even line your refrigerator with wax paper. Molten bees wax can be used for granite surface tops saving money where stains cannot be removed easily.

In foods

Carnauba wax from Brazil is often used in confectionary and food coatings. Paraffin wax can be found in some chocolates and coverings of bonbons. Cheaper chocolate may contain paraffin wax to increase the shelf life and give a shine to the outside of the bar. Bees' wax also helps stop chocolate melting especially useful in hot countries. Wax can harden chocolates and is used for chocolate dips and coatings. Sweets, such as jelly beans and worms and others can contain wax as an ingredient or as coatings. Wax is also found in cakes and pastries and is used as a thickener in sauces, beverages and gravy. It can be a preservative for culinary leaves used in cooking. Chewing gum contains paraffin wax, resins and elastomers and uses hard microcrystalline waxes. Crayons use food grade wax so they can be safe if accidently eaten.

Preservation

The major use of petroleum waxes is in preservation to increase the shelf life. When sprayed on tropical citrus fruits melons, stone fruits, tomatoes, sweet potatoes, avocados, peppers, cucumbers. This prevents oxidation and improves appearance. Only two drops of wax may be all that is used to cover an apple but it may have an antifungal agent included. Some waxes sprayed on may also contain other preservatives. It has been suggested that you use baking soda or Henry Hudson and crew lemon juice to clean the fruit and vegetables before eating. There have been debates on whether wax coatings on fruit or vegetables are Kosher or can be eaten by vegans as they are an animal product, but this brings into question whether honey is Kosher. Wax is also used to cover harder cheeses such as Gouda and Edam. It can be applied by painting or the cheese can be dipped in molten wax. Waxed paper is used to cover cheeses and butters.

Jars can be sealed with wax to prevent dehydration. A layer of wax is placed on the top of jars of jams. Jellies or cheese and butter or a piece of waxed paper is used to help with preservation. Chinese wax is used on dried sausages and waxed paper is placed between burgers. The inside of cartons can also be waxed to prevent air entering or leakage.

Other aspects

Some candles are sold as vegan candles but this does not mean one can eat them. Tallow candles rom animal fats have been eaten. Eating disorders exist where people will have cravings and continue to eat candles to try and relieve stress.

Henry Hudson and crew on their fourth voyage in search for the Northwest Passage ran out of food and eat seagull bones fried in candle wax. The crew were rationed to a pound of candles per week. It is said that a pregnant woman must not eat wax during her pregnancy as her baby when born would be covered in a white coat.

In japan and also in Norway crows have been known to eat tallow candles even taken molten candles wax from graves. It is suggested they are fattening up for winter by eating wax.

12 Hair

Wax can be used in styling and conditioning and also as a hair remover e.g. bikini line. Wax removes facial and body hair. One needs to smooth down hairs in the direction of hair growth, downwards on legs, and then apply wax to the area. It takes a few seconds. Wax only sticks to hairs not the skin. One can use soft wax or strip wax which is like honey when heated for large areas. You can put powder on skin first to prevent pulling. Sugar wax is wax mixed with water, lemon and sugar, applied as a paste and applied like trip wax. One can use it as a paste.

Conditioners which contain wax enhance the volume. The slimy structure and texture does not make hair stiff but stops drying, and prevents breakage. Different strengths can be used for different hair styles. Wax in hair can give a luminous reflection style. You can change the style as it stays flexible so can restyle. The harder the wax the better hold and can even get spiky hair.

Moustache wax has equal parts bees wax and Vaseline. There are also eyebrow wax sprays.

13. INDUSTRY AND WEAPONS

Egyptians used wax for adhesive and shipbuilding. Romans used wax for waterproofing Wax has many uses in industry and in small businesses. Wax is a binder and it sticks well to metal, glass and wood and can be used for making composite logs. The Chandlers Company in the city of London originally made all bees' wax products.

Uses of wax can assist industry. Paraffin wax can reduce friction and prevent corrosion especially for iron. Wax is used on nails and screws to prevent splintering. In building wax can be in found in water repellent composite boards. Wax can also be used as a vacuum sealant and holds down to minus 9 torr at 20 degrees centigrade.

Waxes can also give a matting effect in paint. PVC can be made flame retardant by adding chlorinating paraffin wax. Wax is also included in hot melt adhesives to improve flow and in inks in the printing industry.

Wax can be a seal for concrete surfaces.

The World of Wax

Dipping dead ducks or other birds into bees' wax in hot water allows the wax to solidify on the birds feathers making it easier to pluck them in factories. Paraffin wax has a use in the paper industry to help flow and wax helps with pulling thin precious metal wires and prevents moisture entry by covering electrical components as an insulator.

Wax in tyre and rubber helps to reduce oxidation that can dry out the rubber. Other uses of wax include grinding and polishing lenses. A waterproofing covering using wax is found on matches and wax can be a glossing agent in laundry. Wax moulds are used for release of polyurethane foams.

Wax candles can be recycled by melting down old wax. You need to avoid soya or jelly wax. One can make coloured candles lighter by adding white or cream wax or change colours by adding dyes. Too many colours may produce a dull brown wax. Unscented wax can be used to dilute the scent that was in the candles.

One can remove pieces of wick etc. by heating the wax and allowing debris to settle to the base or remove floating material. One can also cut off the area of the newly set wax where the dirt has settled.

Plain or corrugated waxed cardboard or paper board is used to protect foods or fluid, especially during transportation. Recycling is a problem for milk and juice containers or fast food wrappers. Some papers can be reused for wrapping or papers can be placed in boiling water so that the released wax floats to the top and can be reused for many wax products. One can compost and wax will breakdown after some time but there may be other additives present. Waxed corrugated containers, using paraffin wax can produce good compost and can be biodegraded. Many councils do not recycle wax card or paper and it goes to landfill. It is important to look at new ways of extracting the wax and some industrial processes do now exist for recycling wax and its reuse. Pellets can be made of recycled fibre which is coated with these extracted waxes.

The World of Wax

Other uses of wax include sealing cracks in horse's hooves and the use on dry flies or fishing lines to help them float. Steel tools in the workshop can be protected from rusting.

Beeswax is used to flux lead when casting bullets. This helps remove impurities. Longbows are coated with beeswax and linseed oil wax. In the crusades beeswax of pitch and sulphur were thrown at Christians. Incendiary devices and explosives covered the outside or used to keep components together. Planes and weapons were also covered in wax. Beekeepers were not allowed to go into service at war time.

14. <u>MEDICINE AND DENTISTRY</u>

Bone wax has been used especially for sealing and filling small cavities in bone in the skull and to stop any bleeding. The wax is sterile and used like putty after cutting through bone in an operation. It can be mixed with vaseline and applied with a spatula.
Bees wax had been used for teeth since Roman times. It may be used in temporary fillings, or for crafting dentures. It is also found on dental floss to protect the gums. Wax can also be used for holding items together. Lower and upper jaw impressions can be made on wax which may be a mixture of waxes with other additives or plasticisers.

White wax is used to seal pills in Chinese medicine as well as being a carrier in some pharmaceutical preparations.
Wax can also be used as a base for some anti-inflammatory compounds. Aloe Vera in wax can reduce pain on the face and chocolate crème wax may be anti-inflammatory and can be used as a tablet, a

covering or an ointment. Wax has also been used to cover wounds and cuts as a spray on plaster. Wax protects and repairs dry skin as keeps it moisture in. It also can have anti-swelling effects and act as an antiseptic or for treating fungal infections.

Where corpses were difficult to get hold of, wax was also important for making medical anatomical models (Moulage) for training students. Some of these models are very realistic in shape and colour as they could be painted and parts could be examined. They also could illustrate sores and blisters as well as skin diseases and infection. Many artists were involved in producing these and they can still be found in museums today such as Guys Hospital, London. The Catholic church was often behind the making of anatomical venuses lifelike models. Often these wax figures had beautiful lifelike features .In a church in Salvador de Bahia, Brazil wax sculptures of limbs and body organs are hung on the ceilings. These represent those parts of the body that require healing and the church is believed to provide a cure. In Italy and

Spain it was common if going to the shrine of a saint for healing to leave a small anatomical wax votive.

.

When Marijuana is placed in a pipe with lighter fuel and lit; it leaves a hard waxy active extract. This is marijuana wax which is then placed on a bong or vapouriser and smoked. In this form it is more powerful than marijuana, as is purer and the effect are quicker.

15. MODELLING

Wax provides an excellent media for making models. Eight thousand bricks were made out of it in 2014 and a melting building was constructed by Alex Chinneck in Bankside in London. This was called a pound of flesh for fifty pence. Material can be coated in wax to stop discolouring. Examples are Pysanky folk art, batik and fabric dyeing.

The Victorians liked to keep a likeness of their dead ones and life size models of children were created out of wax. They were fully dressed and were present at the funeral. Even their own hair was used on the model .These figures were then left at the graveside or kept at home and their clothes changed regularly. An alternative for full sized models was the use of models of the diseased head and shoulders mounted in a picture frame.

In the Czech Republic, Poland and Rumania Easter eggs are decorated (Pysanky).Eggs can be covered with bees wax and the wax drawn into the egg shell.

For modelling, people often use microcrystalline wax which is sticky when hot and can melt in the hand. Carving waxes are hard and putty knives and heat guns can be used. One can put wax in the fridge to allow carving. Pouring waxes can be used to connect other pieces together but may also be more brittle. Some waxes are coloured to indicate their properties. Blue indicates the softest wax, whilst purple is medium. Green coloured wax denotes the hardest but is too brittle to use for delicate parts. Blue wax is used by jewellers and one can buy wax with a hole created in the centre for making ring moulds.

Some waxes have plastic in them to make them harder. These can be sandpapered to make them smoother. The lost wax technique for making jewellery goes back to ancient times where the form required is first moulded in wax and then covered with plaster and the wax melted out. Silver or gold is then poured into the mould and the plaster removed. One can make tablets of soap containing wax as an ingredient together with fragrant oils or even flower petals. Medallions can be cast in wax e.g. the

The World of Wax

Renaissance bronze medallions of Pisanello were cast from wax

Kew also has lots of wax models of many plants. Examples include orchids, plant embryos, apples and pears. It also has a model of one of the largest flowers, a life-size Raffleria which is three feet tall. The flowers smell like rotten meat. A model of a gigantic water lily held in Kew was sculptured in wax and presented to Queen Victoria and Prince Albert. Queen Victoria had ten thousand wax roses made for her wedding.

Wax models of meals and other food items are often found in the widows of Japanese restaurants.

In the past letters were folded as there were no envelopes and the pages were sealed with wax

Documents sealed with sealing wax could have a stamp or ring used to make an impression on the wax. The seal could have an impression on both sides with a ribbon through the middle. For ceremonial documents, charters etc. different coloured seals were used. Red was common but green was used for court documents and was used by the Black Prince. Black wax was used for mourning letters. A German emperor used white wax for seals.

Beeswax can also be modelled in charms. Charms can be made in a form that can bring bad effects on enemies as well as for protection to the wearer. Some tribes in Australia and South America use wax to model familiar animals. One South America tribe makes whistles out of wax.

Wax models in Ancient Egypt were believed to have magical and religious properties. Wax models of humans and animals (shabtis) are found inside mummy wrappings.

Soft toys can be dipped in wax and the excess is squeezed out. Their fur can then be roughed up and their heads can be positioned in any direction before the wax sets. Fragrances can also be added to the wax.

16. MUSIC AND FILM

Wax is often used in instruments to ensure a good seal. In oboes in Egypt wax was placed in unneeded finger holes. In bagpipes wax is used to protect the rims of the bagpipe joints. In accordions beeswax is used to make a good seal around the brads that attach the bellows. The head of an oboe can be waxed before the reed is inserted. The didgeridoo can have the mouth piece waxed.

Some instruments use wax to strengthen thin parchment. The surfaces of tambourines, drums combs and reeds for woodwind instruments are examples.

A wax coating on instruments, especially stringed, will increase their longevity. This protects the varnish from any acids produced and sticky rosin from violins etc. Research has gone on to determine the best waxed formulation to use which is long-lasting.

Playing the comb uses the same method as a kazoo using wax paper. Waxed paper is folded over the comb and held across the teeth with the comb pointing down. This is then placed against your lips and by saying "Ooooooooooo"to get a buzz sound the air frequency causes the paper to vibrate and make a tingling feeling on the lips. Drumsticks can also be coated in wax give a tacky grip.

Alexander Bell and Charles Tainter established wax on cylinders as a recording method where a cutting stylus etches a groove. The speed of rotation was slower for voice and faster for music
 As opposed to just making an indentation, as the Edison's tinfoil phonograph had done.
Several bands contain the name wax in them. The May Swanson band is called Wax. There is also a wax band in los Angelis called Wax which is a park rock/punk rock band.

Music referring to wax.

A Sailors Tale - (Musical) by William Shield, Benjamin Carr is based on scenes from The Odyssey. The oarsmen and rest of the crew had wax in their ears Odysseus wishes to hear the sirens but is tied to the mast so he cannot be diverted to where the creatures live

Blood and Crisps- Banging on Wax. volume. 2.

Cho Hye-Ri - goes by the name wax. –A South Korean pop star/ actor performing in a musical 'Fixing My Makeup'.

Elton John -Candle in the Wind was sung at the Diana's funeral.

Chris Young -Twenty one candles.

Hymn -Jesus shall reign whe're the sun- 'his kingdom stretch from shore to shore till moons shall wax and wane no more'.

Irish song –'The water is wide but love grows old and waxes cold and fades away like the morning dew'.

Jim Boyd -doghouse Waxachachie boogiee woogie dishwasher boy.

J T. Money -Pimpin on wax album.

Jeremy Mc Kinnon- I'm made of wax, Larry what are you made of?

Joshua Radin- Album Wax Wings.

Longfellow –'the moon will wax the moon will wane, the mist and cloud will turn to rain'.

Moniker Wax Mannequin -name adopted by Chris Adeney second album 'and gun' portrayed with candle on his head and wax dripping down his face.

Peter Paul and Mary –'puff the magic dragon and brought him strings and sealing wax and other fancy stuff'.

Peter Paul and Mary -Light one Candle.

Raashan Ahmad -In Love with Wax.

Rolling stones -19th nervous breakdown. 'Your mother who neglected you owes a million. dollars tax and your father's still perfecting ways of making sealing. wax'.

Wax Organix-uses synthesizers and sequencers and live songs improvised. Played at the Longwoodstock beer and music festival.

Wax music recording Studio based in Stratford, East London.

City of Wax 1934 Life of a Bee.

House of Wax. (Film 1953 and 2005) Realistic wax figures are actual people. A fight to survive against two brothers.

Mystery of the wax museum 1933

Pink string and sealing wax 1945

The man with Wax Faces 1914

The Ring of Wax. Batman TV episode. 1966.

Wax Princess. 4th and final audio story in the 7th

season of Jago and Lightfoot. 2014.

17. NAMES

The wax surname is first recorded first in Middlesex as the lord of the manor with a coat of arms. Family names containing the word wax include Wax, Waxman, Waxmonger, Waxande, and Waxing. Ruby Wax is a presenter and comic who has received an OBE for her role as a mental health campaigner.

Some animals have wax in their names. A bird's name with wax in it is the waxbill belonging to the finch family. The name originates from its bright red bill which resembles red sealing wax. Another bird is the silvereye or wax eye bird from New Zealand. It is olive green with a ring of white feathers around its eye.

The waxwing is a reddish-brown, black throated plump bird, which is slightly smaller than a starling. It has a prominent crest.

Wax worms or bee moths are members of the snout moth family. They are the caterpillar larvae of wax moths. There are several close species. As caterpillars they bore through the bees wax and eat pollen and the bee young. Two closely related species are commercially bred – the lesser wax moth (Achroia grisella) and the greater wax moth (Galleria mellonella).

Wax beans are yellow coloured. They taste like string beans can be eaten cooked or raw and are commonly known as butter beans.

Places in UK with wax in their names.

Shropshire-Wax hall.

Norfolk-Waxham.

Yorkshire Waxhol

Devon-Waxway.

18. PRESERVATION AND PROTECTION

Many things can be preserved using wax. Waxed paper has many uses and wax is also put into or on card to strengthen or make it water resistant, as well as making it more flexible. Wax in packaging is in major use worldwide, much more than wax being used for candles. Cheese and butter can be kept in paraffin wax paper as well as wax paper being used on jars of jams.

Wax paper stops fabric colours from fading in light. Carbon paper has a coating of wax on one side which captures the writing or type. Wax is used on the back of hanging scrolls in China and paper kites and model aeroplanes, and boats can be waterproofed. Waxed rope can be made of many materials and have different uses related to protection, waterproofing and lubrication. Examples include marine ropes, ranch ropes for horses, sash window rope and ropes used on pulleys.

The World of Wax

Waxed cotton was widely used up to 1950's. Paraffin wax was incorporated into the threads on the cloth. Its use on threads helps to water proof, strengthen or hold frayed ends together in place. Waxed thread is used to join materials which are exposed to rain or other tough conditions. Examples include leather, bradings, umbrellas, camping and marine materials. Irish waxed linen cord is often used for jewelry and deigns. Candlewick embroidery as seen in bedspreads used a white yarn that was also used for the wick of candles.

Waxed Egyptian cotton was originally used in sails in preference to applying oils for sailing. Initially linseed oil was used but in the cold the material became rigid. Capes were made from pieces of waxed sail. Cotton impregnated with wax still is common in outdoor county clothing for farmers and motorcyclists. Waxed cotton jackets and textiles are common but the fabric is not very breathable. This was replaced by paraffin wax treatment and now refined hydrocarbons wax are used which reduces the smell.

Wax can be used to extend the life of cut flowers .This is especially useful where you want to save flowers from a bridal event or even a funeral. Good flowers for waxing include roses, daisies, lilies and orchids, and those which already have some natural waxy coating or thicker petals. Do not use wilting flowers. Before dipping you need to remove damaged petals. Molten wax is held in a water bath and excess wax allowed to run off the dipped flower. To ensure the flower is fully waxed wax can be spooned into its centre. One can dip the stem into the wax, once the head has been dipped and its wax set.

Dipped flowers can be hung upside down on pegs on a string line or placed into the open top of a bottle. Once the wax is dry the flower will last several months without discolouring. If kept in the dark and kept dry they could last for many years.
Wax can be used for waxing pine needle baskets. Melted wax is applied using a foam brush. The wax stiffens the basket and protects the threads.

The World of Wax

Wax use for protection and sealing is seen for corks in jars and bottles and water containers. Leather goods such as shoes, boots, whips and saddles. are protected by wax. Wax needs to get right into the leather. Bees wax and turpentine will fill all pores. In order to get a fine shine it is good to some add water before wax polishing. Without wax water can enter and remove the tanning agent and make the leather stiffer.

Glass etching involves coating the glass with bees wax and making a design through it. The glass is then etched using acid. Marble is easily stained by contact with coloured liquids which can sink into the surface. Without coating first with wax, removing the stain would usually require re-grinding to eliminate the marks. Many statues and monuments in city streets are now protected from weathering, corrosion and oxidation by wax. Arms, armour, steel and kitchen equipment of brass and copper in historic house museums are kept bright and corrosion-free by coating with wax.

As well as a rust protector, wax can act as a lubricator e.g. to help release stuck zipper teeth, lubricate saws, bolts and other workshop tools. Even the bottom of irons can be waxed to prevent them from sticking. There is a shuffleboard wax which is like baby powder and reduced friction so that pucks can travel along the shuffleboard tables. Small diameter wood drills can be dipped into wax to help eliminate drill breakage when working on hard woods. Blacksmiths can finishes off iron work by coating it with wax. This gives sheen and prevents rust. Bronze statues can be waxed using a stiff hair brush followed by a soft cloth.

As a polisher wax can be used on concrete surfaces. Repeated use of wax does not affect clarity but enhances the lustre making a shiny surface and the fine detail remains. A thin layer of wax on cars or boats provides protection from ultra violet light so as to reduce fading of the paint and helps water run-off. In hot weather it can melt and evaporate within six weeks. It is useful to put on wax before winter starts to protect the body work from abrasion and grit.

The World of Wax

Where chalk paints are used on furniture wax can be applied on top and the wax buffed up. Beams in houses can be waxed to preserve them. Some waxes contain acids which in time could spoils original finishes on historic collections of furniture. Crayons can be used to retouch furniture. Wax is used to help in releasing drawers in furniture, open windows, and metal file cabinet's doors.

There are lots of other uses of wax. It can be used to fill holes where slate was used for billiard tables. Bees' wax balls are used for oil spills. The balls contain microorganisms that digest the oil.

Rosin in a wax mixture can be used for waxing bow strings for stringed instruments and archery bows. In magic tricks wax mixed with rosin and oils gives mystic smoke when rubbed. The smoke appears to come from the fingers.

19. SPORT AND SCIENCE

Wax in sport is linked to reducing friction and helping increase speed. Wax on skis acts as a sealant and a lubricant. Without it skis may not slide at all. Chemicals can be added to the wax to reduce the friction.

Wax can be applied 1-3 times a month or more for professional use. Before application one needs to dry the area and put wax on runners. Candle wax is sometimes successful. The amount of water under the skis etc. has an effect. Too much water creates drag, and too little causes dry fiction. Glide wax and grip wax are influenced by the type of snow and temperature. A harder glide wax with fluorine or other solids e.g. Teflon gives good water repellency. Cross- country skiing uses grip wax chosen for different temperatures for traction. It is useful for going forward on hills and the flat especially when weight is put on one ski.

The World of Wax

Cross country skiers use grip wax to give traction when going forward on hills and late grip wax is for different temperatures and snow types.

Wax is also used for sectioning animal and plant tissues. The water in the cell is replaced with alcohol then with toluol or xylene. The tissue is then placed in paraffin wax which enters the cells. This wax prevents damage when the tissue is cut into thin sections with a razor sharp microtome. The sections are dewaxed and stained for looking under the microscope. Plastic petri-dishes, flasks and viles are sealed with parafilm sealing wax to stop organisms entering or leaving the media carrying contamination.

20. WORDS AND SAYINGS

<u>Packwax</u> is a strong ligament in the neck.

Wax apples are bell shaped fruits from Asia with watermelon like centres. Contain a lot of tannin.

<u>Waxberry</u> is a common name for several plants examples a white waxberry from Australia, the candleberry from North America, and the snowberry a genus of the honeysuckle family.

<u>Waxplant</u> is one that produces wax which can be harvested.

<u>Wax play</u> is where one covers someone in drips hot wax which can be various colours. The person can be tied up first. There is a slight burning sensation felt but you may need a sharp knife to remove the wax afterwards.

<u>Wax turnips</u> Rutabagas. Are a cross between a turnip and a cabbage coated with paraffin wax.

<u>Woadwaxen or woodwaxen</u> is a small Eurasian shrub with yellow flowers common in United Kingdom and the United States that gives yellow dye.

<u>Wood waxes</u> are polishes put on to protect wood or can be a mushroom feeding on beech or oak.

Other waxy words

Dewaxing, rewaxing, waxed, ,waxen, unwaxed, waxable, waxes, waxers, waxier, waxiest, waxiness, waxing, waxings, waxiness, waxlike, waxsmith, waxwork, waxworkers.

Sayings

Many other slang expressions refer to sexual context

Mind your own beeswax its none of your beeswax -means none of your business Also may be linked to staring at someone's face after small pox or bees wax would melt if close to the fire.

Good girls wax their floors while bad girls wax their bikini line.

Wax - (in 1950's) a vinyl record (LP).

Wax (and waned) -increase in size or number strength or intensity or to defeat completely. We waxed the competition.

Waxxa- is used in the north east of England. Some people refer to a good thing as being this.

Wax angry -is to speak angrily and with indignity.

Wax argument or the ball of wax- is an experiment on thought by Rene Descartes on the uncertainty of our knowledge of the world.

Waxwing Crackas -is the most dangerous of the gangs that reside in East Amherst who are involved in illegal activities and armed.

Wax eloquently -increasingly expansive and expressive in speech.

Wax a gaza- is to climb up a gas lamp telling someone to go away.

Waxier -is a male who waxes his eyebrows or an insult without swearing.

Wax lyrical -is talking enthusiastically about something.

Wax nostalgic -talking about nostalgia.

Wax on /wax off -phrase from the Karate Kid. Refers to circular hand motions.

Wax philosophical -means growing increasingly strong or intense in a certain direction, in this case in philosophical insight.

<u>Wax poetic</u>- is to speak poetically and with authority on something for a long period.

<u>Wax political</u>- is talking about politics.

<u>Wax preachers-</u>African/American protestant preachers old time sermons on wax recordings

<u>Wax the cat</u>- is to clean the pubic area.

<u>Wax whore</u>- is a woman who gets a bikini wax anywhere and from anyone.

<u>Other books by Mike Pearce:</u>

1. Pattern for Purpose- God's and Man's designs
2. Red Fred Cell and Friends
3. Human Termites eat London
4. Pigeons Splat London
5. Glass Anemones Tentacle-ize London
6. Tuppeny Hangover
7. I am Termite
8. The littlest Oyster
9. Bits and Bobs
10. The Shell Man
11. Cats at Christmas
12. Tails, Tales
13. Trust-Nothing but a Must
14. In a Dark, Dark Corner was the Holy Ghost
15. The shell lady
16. Captain Grottbuster versus the Grey World
17. London's Nemesis(Trilogy of 3,4 and 5 above
18. Saved by Angels (Trilogy of 6,8 and 14 above)

MIKE PEARCE

ABOUT THE AUTHOR

Dr Mike Pearce is a scientist interested in behaviour. He also was a lecturer in human biology and health at a college in Canterbury, Kent

www.ingramcontent.com/pod-product-compliance
Lightning Source LLC
Chambersburg PA
CBHW071221280526
45787CB00002B/754